T0132412

Being a Twin

A Reflection

Timothy Nichols

AuthorHouse™
1663 Liberty Drive
Bloomington, IN 47403
www.authorhouse.com
Phone: 1 (800) 839-8640

Published by AuthorHouse 09/06/2018

ISBN: 978-1-5246-7573-8 (sc)
ISBN: 978-1-5246-7574-5 (e)

Library of Congress Control Number: 2017907342

Print information available on the last page.

Any people depicted in stock imagery provided by Thinkstock are models,
and such images are being used for illustrative purposes only.
Certain stock imagery © Thinkstock.

This book is printed on acid-free paper.

Because of the dynamic nature of the Internet, any web addresses or links contained in this book may have changed
since publication and may no longer be valid. The views expressed in this work are solely those of the author and do not
necessarily reflect the views of the publisher, and the publisher hereby disclaims any responsibility for them.

Cover Photo taken by Peoble Divers / Peoble Photography

authorHOUSE®

Dedication

This book is in dedication to my brother Tom Nichols.

S etting is Welcome Minnesota. It was a high school football game. Our team was from Alden Minnesota. The team did not have a lot of what I will call smaller athletes to carry the ball so we both had duty to do this for both kickoff and punt returns. The game was close.

Being in Minnesota, half way to South Dakota, on the prairie, start of winter, it was bone chilling. We had key kickoff returns to get the team far enough to make another score. When we walked out to the field we already knew our role. Instead of talking of strategy of a return we both talked about what each of us would do that night after the game. At that point the game was more mechanical for us. In a very heightened sports environment we always found a way to converse and stand up for each other.

I was a regular running back. My brother Tom was excellent at returning kickoffs for touchdowns. If they tried to kick it to me, I would hand the ball off to him and run forward ahead to pick off anyone I could to keep them out of his way. The head blasts might have an effect on me in older age!

I am an identical twin. I thought I would put together a book for reflection of past stories of being one. This is not a statistical theory of how twins are similar or dissimilar, but rather just some good stories on experiences that I had with mine.

Yes, we looked like each other. And we did all sports together, even had most school classes together. Our interests were similar. We didn't necessarily have the same friends. That is one reason I did not want to do a statistical analysis on this. I don't believe in this theory. Twins are siblings, but they do not share the same brain.

Early Alden Days

The Nichols house was right on the lake in the center of Alden. We spent time catching and being stung by "bullheads". We were little kids, it was just something to do. We also were around other ones close by. The Wesley house, with Mike, Sue, and Renae, having to put up with us. This was when we first learned how to ride a bicycle. After living there the Nichols picked up to the east side of town.

At that time, being identical twins, you really couldn't tell each of us apart. We had a common name of "Tim Tom". That way no matter the name it worked. The bike riding back to the lake in later years to catch as many bullheads as possible and riding back to east Alden to consume came in handy. I couldn't eat them but the Newman families on the street loved to make fish fries of them. If I had one I just needed a lot of ketchup to blunt the taste!

Sports were an artifact of the Nichols household from a young age. The above photo from the Albert Lea Tribune captured two little goofballs walking home from school. The reporter had something else to cover but saw us, pulled over, and snapped a picture for the paper. The caps were Minnesota Vikings, the patches were both Vikings and a professional hockey team in St. Paul called the Fighting Saints. There were also homecoming buttons for the local Alden-Conger school. I was even carrying a Viking program.

Wrestling Days

The above picture is me and Tom with Coach Nelson. We must have been waiting for a wrestling tournament run. Setting is Kiester-Walters Christmas tournament. It is either eighth or ninth grade.

Since we were in sports many times together, we also had many common friends in wrestling. We got along with each other and everyone that also did battle with us. The picture below is of a common friend, whom is still in contact with me, of a wrestling teammate, Craig Johnson. Tom and I were always close in the weight classes but Craig Johnson would sometimes "clock" some of the ones that would create havoc on me and him. Yes that is me trying to flip off the camera! Craig and his close friend Darrin Savoy would always look out for us. As in a team we all had a common goal to do the best we can for all around us, to win, and win in life.

The setting for the picture below is in front of the Kiester-Walters High School trophy section. They are now part of a school district called United South Central. I still have a good friend, Troy Ranum from Walters. He has connected with me to come down to the Albert Lea Legion on a Sunday for a pancake. I am two hours' drive away! I remember I told him I will be right there! He battled both me and Tom over our wrestling years.

There is a point with wrestlers that they have a lot of respect for each other. It is a tough sport. It goes beyond the mat. Troy and his company of friends were the first to come to Tom's wake when he left us.

Both me and Tom could embrace each other's ups and recognize and feel the downs. I remember seeing him lose a wrestling match for getting to the Minnesota state tournament in the last few seconds. This was in seventh grade. In the state of Minnesota seventh graders can wrestle at the high school level. It was heartbreaking. He never spoke of this the rest of his life. It was not something I would ever bring up with him. It was not a thing he thought of being important, he thought of moving forward and being with family and friends as he was getting older.

Tom was the one being "groomed" to be a wrestler. I initially chose basketball. Either sport would be alright with me. When the wrestling team had some weight spots to fill they asked me to step in for one. I accepted. I remember Coach Nelson asking me if I would be comfortable doing this. It was an easy answer for me. Tom has already done this and I am athletic I will learn quickly. I had "little" brother for advice.

The timeframe now is eighth grade. Tom was the lowest in the weight class. I was one or two up weight class wise in a match depending on how Coach wanted to position myself. When we reached tenth grade I had a major sickness and dropped so much weight in a summer we switched who was the lower and higher in weights. Tom took this in stride. He would end up putting up with much larger ones that at that point I did not.

I ended up being the one to make the Minnesota state tournament runs. Tom never did. When I was a likely one in our senior year, and lost, I was pretty upset with myself. He was the first to understand and do what he could to make me happy. I don't remember exactly but he may have said words like we do have baseball left to play. That is all I needed to pick me up.

Baseball Days

Another sport we had in common was baseball. The weird thing of this is that he batted right, and I batted left. Our father must have set this one up when we were very young. It worked out good for me. When growing up left handed batters were far a few between. That meant the batters box for a left handed batter was usually in pristine shape. Sorry Tom!

We both played ball through the whole system where we grew up. Sometimes playing outfield, then the Alden-Conger high school baseball coach Neil Pierce asked for me to play third base. Tom played both second base and shortstop. Again, we followed each other. We also played American Legion baseball together over the years. We both held several different positions but were happy to play.

The picture above is Tom on the left and me on the right. The Nichols house is in the background. Being ball players we spent a lot of time on this field. The funny thing about this picture is that Tom was a right handed batter, and I was lefty, even though the bat was held by me as a righty for this picture. We had numbers one and two, and the other two in our class on this team, Jay Jensen and Steve Sanderson, took three and four. We all carried these numbers in our high school times through our senior year.

This was sent to me from Tom from in his Mankato State days to myself at Wisconsin-Stout, trying to convince me to transfer to his college. I did think about it but just couldn't pull the trigger on that one. I was well along in a good program in college and was happy with it. At this time we still kept contact the best we could before internet time. It was letters or visiting each other in person at each other's colleges. The point was he would have liked to have me close by and thought it would make me happier.

New York Days

We both ended our college days, mine going to New York to work for IBM. Tom was having a tough time getting work in the Twin Cities so I invited him out to New York. I had an empty bedroom so why not. And he did. He also ended up working for IBM. He was accepted as part of the family of friends that I was already a part.

We did many things together. Two shy young men that found their way to New York being computer professionals. We would go to local friends' homes to help with whatever the task was at hand. We helped one of my department team lead engineer help out with a new house. The big thing was a walk down to the Hudson river in the fall. The leaves were up to our knees. So far ok. When we got back up the hill we were warned of the rattler snakes that we walked through. We were both freaked out at that point. Snakes were never a welcome theme with me and Tom.

By then I had already established myself as an ok IBM softball coach and led a team of friends, all computer "geeks, myself included. Tom was also on the team and worked odd shifts and barely would make it to games on time. By then I gave him the nickname of "Smokey" for a stray dog that ran around the city of Alden. When he would make it one minute before a game and I had him bat way up in the order, so he basically was running to the batters box out of the car. The IBM team would just chant "hit one out Smokey"! He would turn and glare at me while I held the scorebook at third base and just laughed.

Tom and I would go to local bars for a drink. Before the dish days, some places would have satellite dishes. The owner of one bar liked to pan around for something good to put on the monitors. When he was panning once, he crossed a Minnesota Gopher and Kansas Jayhawk basketball game. Immediately Tom said, stop, I want to watch the Kansas game. The owner thought you are right, Kansas is good. He really just wanted to watch the Gophers!

When Tom came to New York he needed to get another car. I went with him to a used car dealership in Poughkeepsie. He was looking around the lot for one. One of the sons, I think, came out and was giving prices on the spot for each vehicle. At once this person gave a price, and Tom said "I'll take it". At that point the dealer said maybe the price wasn't right. I was there and told the fellow that is a verbal and binding contract. I was witness to it. He got the car. I had his back covered on that one.

For about three years he worked at his IBM facility, and I did as well in a different one. When I was getting ready to transfer back to Minnesota for IBM I needed a place to stay for a week so I stayed with him. It was a townhome with no basement. He just told me if you hear a really loud pickup truck going through the area it is just the married woman's husband looking for where I live, having a relationship with me. He said don't worry it is me not you! What! Thanks a lot Tom!

Travels to Minnesota

One of the interesting and funny things we had together were our travels back and forth from New York to Minnesota. It was mainly in winter Christmas time. For something happening on the road it seemed to be a recurrent theme.

One time traveling back to New York we had to pull off the road in Janesville Wisconsin. We got the last hotel room available. It was not fun driving. It was just good to be off the road and safe for a night. I don't remember a fast food place close by of the hotel. That story is next. We were safe, made a good part of the trip already, and just enjoyed talking and being with each other.

Tom always wanted to do the plane trips back for friends and family. I had to tell him not to do it. There are so many places we could drive together and stop and enjoy and chat with people. Boy that may have been a mistake!

Working for IBM during and after college in New York, I had already made these travel runs. When driving to a point in need of rest I had two places I would always stop. One was Lock Haven in Pennsylvania. Another was Elkhart Indiana. I don't know if this is a Nichols travel thing but something always would happen. I did one alone, with no stops outside of gas, with a six pack of Jolt pop and beat a winter storm heading to Minnesota. Our mother was not happy with me!

One time staying in Elkhart I phoned home to say I would be there in the morning. Dad said why aren't you staying for the Notre Dame game? That wasn't on my mind. Our parents had a tradition to make it to an Irish game there next door every year. Sorry, I am just coming home.

The picture above is Dad in his "perch". He loved to watch his boys play baseball and football from it. I can't remember a time that sports were not part of the family. He would take us to the old Bloomington stadiums of Twins, and North Stars. We loved it.

As I mentioned we made many trips together from New York to Minnesota. The main corridor was Interstate 80 going out west. We tried to make it through without stops. One time trying to get back for Christmas we really didn't have a choice. In the middle of Pennsylvania we ran in to a sleet storm. Tom was driving, there was an exit close by at the bottom of the hill. Many vehicles were going into the ditch, including at least one semi. I just told him pull off, we can wait this out before morning. That was the beginning of an interesting night.

We got off the interstate and actually got the last room in a hotel. So far so good. There was a band playing in the hotel downstairs so we thought while we are stuck here lets get some entertainment and have something to eat. The band was so bad I lost my appetite for eating and just asked Tom can we not eat here. He was "Heck yah, lets go over the parking lot to McDonalds." Still, so far so good.

The travel from New York to Minnesota, and back, in winter always had a high probability of running in to rough weather. There were times, before internet days where you just did not know when bad weather would happen. We did the same being stuck in Janesville Wisconsin on a trip back to New York. Me and Tom made the best of this.

Back to middle Pennsylvania. When we were in lines about ten lengths long with everyone and their grandmother getting off the interstate, Tom made his order first. The funniness then started.

Tom was at the counter and ordered two hamburgers and out loud, asked for a "fish burger". Everyone heard him. I couldn't hide from this. He knew the whole place was looking at him. He turned around and just said "how we all doing?", in the biggest southern drawl he could come with. What do you do at this point, I can't say I am not with him, I look just like him

An old gentleman walked up to him and poked him and asked, "You aint from around you are you?". Without a plause he responded "Heck no, I am from that there Ioway place". At that point do you laugh, hide, no can't do that, still have an appetite? No. That was Tom. At that point the point the food was not important. He fed me with a story for life.

I made the escape from New York back to Minnesota. He followed within a year. Both working for IBM. In the next few years we also were married and had kids. Again, we were close. Both in the New York Days and in Rochester Minnesota, we played softball on many teams. In the New York times we each had about three teams each we played. One I was able to get him to play with, and another he had one I played with.

Final

There are times you always will have a memory of something. We all do. I will go back to the Welcome kickoff return with my brother. It was very unpleasant weather. We both knew it. But we found a way to get over the external environment and did not let it affect our goal to win. We shared a common goal in life. We laughed together. We helped each other as best that we could, for kids and family.

Tom and Tim Nichols, age three.

Printed in the United States
By Bookmasters